CHICAGO
CUBS

by George Castle

SportsZone
An Imprint of Abdo Publishing
www.abdopublishing.com

www.abdopublishing.com

Published by Abdo Publishing, a division of ABDO, PO Box 398166, Minneapolis, Minnesota 55439. Copyright © 2015 by Abdo Consulting Group, Inc. International copyrights reserved in all countries. No part of this book may be reproduced in any form without written permission from the publisher. SportsZone™ is a trademark and logo of Abdo Publishing.

Printed in the United States of America, North Mankato, Minnesota
052014
092014

Editor: Chrös McDougall
Copy Editor: Nicholas Cafarelli
Interior Design and Production: Kazuko Collins
Cover Design: Christa Schneider

Photo Credits: Mark Duncan/AP Images, cover; Photo File/MLB Photos via Getty Images, 1; John Bazemore/AP Images, 4, 43 (bottom); Morry Gash/AP images, 7; Jonathan Daniel/Getty Images, 9; National Baseball Hall of Fame Library/MLB Photos via Getty Images, 10, 15, 42 (top and bottom); FPG/Getty Images, 13; AP Images, 16, 19, 21, 23, 24, 27, 42 (middle); Isaac Sutton/Ebony Collection via AP Images, 29, 43 (top); Focus on Sport/Getty Images, 31; John Swart, FILE/AP Images, 32; Mark Elias/AP Images, 35; Mark A. Duncan/AP Images, 36, 43 (middle); Brian Kersey/AP Images, 39; Al Behrman/AP Images, 41; Kent Horner/AP Images, 44; Charles Rex Arbogast/AP Images, 47

Library of Congress Control Number: 2014932904
Cataloging-in-Publication Data
Castle, George.
  Chicago Cubs / by George Castle.
     p. cm. — (Inside MLB)
  Includes bibliographical references and index.
  ISBN 978-1-62403-464-0
  1. Chicago Cubs (Baseball team)—History—Juvenile literature. I. Title.
  GV875.C6C25 2015
  796.357′640977311—dc23
                          2014932904

TABLE OF CONTENTS

CHAPTER 1

BREAKING THE CURSE?

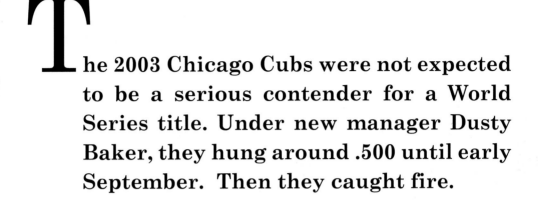

T he 2003 Chicago Cubs were not expected to be a serious contender for a World Series title. Under new manager Dusty Baker, they hung around .500 until early September. Then they caught fire.

A pitching staff led by Mark Prior and Kerry Wood suddenly became one of the best in Major League Baseball (MLB). After some inconsistency, the Cubs' lineup became more productive, too. The Cubs started September by going 8–1. As the month—and season—came to a close, they were right in the mix for the National League (NL) Central Division title.

Extra Support

On July 23, 2003, the Cubs landed third baseman Aramis Ramirez and center fielder Kenny Lofton from the Pittsburgh Pirates for third baseman Jose Hernandez and two minor leaguers. Ramirez and Lofton sparked the Cubs to within five outs of the World Series. Lofton hit .327 with a .381 on-base percentage in 56 games. Ramirez had 15 home runs and drove in 39 runs in 63 games. Lofton left the team after the 2003 season. Ramirez went on to star in Chicago for several years.

Mark Prior reacts after getting an out in Game 2 of the 2003 NL Championship Series against the Florida Marlins.

The Cubs had a chance to win that title on the second-to-last day of the season. They were hosting the Pittsburgh Pirates in a doubleheader at Wrigley Field. When the Cubs won both games, they were division champions. They were heading to the playoffs for the first time since 1998.

The playoffs, however, were not known to be good to the Cubs. The team from Chicago's North Side had not won a play-off series since winning the 1908 World Series. Some fans believed the Cubs could never win another World Series. That is according to a curse supposedly put on the team during the 1945 World Series. When a fan and his goat were kicked out of a game because the goat smelled, he supposedly said the Cubs would never win another World Series.

Curse or no curse, the Cubs got off to a good start. They edged the Atlanta Braves three games to two in the NL Division Series (NLDS). Then they met the Florida Marlins in the NL Championship Series (NLCS).

Cubs fans were starting to feel good about the team's chances. They had a 22–10 record since September 1. Then they took a three-games-to-one lead over the Marlins in the NLCS. Many fans and media

The Curse

On October 6, 1945, the Cubs hosted the Detroit Tigers at Wrigley Field in Game 4 of the World Series. Cubs fan William "Billy Goat" Sianis bought two tickets for the game: one for him, and one for his goat Murphy. However, Sianis and Murphy were ordered to leave because the goat smelled bad. When Sianis was leaving, he reportedly said, "The Cubs ain't gonna win no more. The Cubs will never win a World Series so long as the goat is not allowed in Wrigley Field." The Cubs have not been back to a World Series since.

Cubs outfielder Moises Alou is unable to catch a foul ball when a fan, in headphones, deflects it during Game 6 of the 2003 NLCS.

members felt the Cubs were on the verge of returning to their first World Series since 1945.

The Marlins beat the Cubs 4–0 in Game 5. Then the Cubs hosted the Marlins in Game 6 on the evening of October 14. Prior held a 3–0 lead with one out in the eighth. Then Marlins second baseman Luis Castillo hit what looked like a routine foul ball down toward the left-field box seats. Cubs left fielder Moises Alou leaped against the wall to try to catch the foul pop. Several Cubs fans tried to grab it, too.

The ball deflected off one fan's hands. Alou was unable to catch it and record the second out. The outfielder threw a fit. Cubs fans were not happy

KERRY WOOD

Kerry Wood impressed Cubs fans not only with his strikeouts but also his determination. In spite of repeated shoulder injuries, he always tried to come back. In the spring of 2007, however, his shoulder pain did not improve. "I was one day away from quitting," Wood said.

The pitcher said he was going to tell the team he would retire and undergo surgery when his physical therapist suggested he try throwing again. "He said why not just throw again to flare it up, make sure he [the surgeon] doesn't miss anything?" Wood said. "I went to throw to make it hurt. It felt good."

Wood came back to pitch in the final two months of 2007. Then he saved 34 games as Cubs closer in 2008. Wood later pitched for the Cleveland Indians and the New York Yankees. But he was one of the most popular players in recent Cubs history.

either. The fan had to be escorted out of the stadium by security for his safety.

The Cubs then began to unravel. Shortstop Alex Gonzalez bobbled a ground ball that could have been turned into a double play to get the Cubs out of the inning. Before long, the Marlins had scored eight runs to steal Game 6.

The next night, Wood slugged a homer to thrill the crowd. But he did not have his best stuff on the mound. The Marlins completed the startling comeback with a 9–6 victory. Then they went on to beat the New York Yankees in the World Series.

"I think they drained their tanks for us," Cubs pitching coach Larry Rothschild said of Wood and Prior. "It's the first time either one of them has pitched this long. Now they tasted it, so hopefully in the

Kerry Wood is taken out of Game 7 of the 2003 NLCS after he gave up seven earned runs in 5⅔ innings. The Marlins went on to win 9–6.

future this helps and we can take the next couple steps."

The fans were stunned and depressed. At the same time, they were inspired. The Cubs had a young team in 2003. Many felt they were in a position to return to the NLCS and even the World Series in 2004. Wood was even featured on a 2004 *Sports Illustrated* cover that predicted the Cubs would win that year's World Series by beating the Yankees.

But alas, they did not. After contending throughout the season, the Cubs fell apart. They lost five of their final seven games and missed the playoffs. The Cubs never lived up to their high expectations of finally returning to the World Series. Many Cubs fans still blame it on the curse.

CHAPTER 2

BECOMING THE CUBS

The National Association of Professional Base Ball Players began in 1871 as the first professional baseball league. The Chicago White Stockings played in that league in 1871, 1874, and 1875. However, the league had many problems with gambling and losing games on purpose.

So, in 1876, White Stockings owner William A. Hulbert led a group that formed the National League of Professional Base Ball Clubs.

The National League (NL) began with eight teams. The entrance fee for each team was $100. The NL set out to have better, fairer business practices among the teams. One way they did that was by giving players contracts so they could not be unfairly lured away from their teams.

Each NL team played three games per week for a total of 70 games. The White Stockings played their first game in the league on April 25, 1876. It was a 4–0 victory over the Louisville Grays.

Frank Chance plays catch before a game. He played in Chicago from 1898 to 1912.

"The ball was the deadest possible to be found," the *Chicago Tribune* reported. "The ground was not in good shape and was moist, sticky, and soft in the outfield, and soggy all over."

The White Stockings captured the first NL pennant with a 52–14 record. Albert Spalding was the team's manager. He was also the only full-time pitcher. He had a 47–12 record that season.

The White Stockings remained one of the top teams in the NL. In fact, they won five pennants between 1880 and 1886. However, a players' revolt over salaries in 1890 forced some changes. When 12 players left for a new league, the team had to replace them with some younger players. The team still had many young players in 1902, which led a local newspaper to refer to the team as

Base Ball

"*Base ball*" in 1876 looked much different from today's game. Pitchers threw underhanded, like a bowler, from just 45 feet (13.7 m) on flat ground. The batter could request a high or low pitch. No lineup changes could be made after the fourth inning. A walk required nine balls. Foul balls were not considered strikes. However, a foul caught on the first bounce was an out.

the Cubs. The team officially adopted the name in 1907.

In 1906, the Cubs emerged as the best team in baseball. In fact, they won a record 116 games. Only the 2001 Seattle Mariners have ever matched that feat, although the Mariners played seven more games. The 1906 Cubs won the pennant by 20 games. They led the NL in hitting, pitching, and fielding.

Mordecai Brown was 26–6 with a 1.04 earned run average (ERA) and nine shutouts. Jack

Cubs pitcher Mordecai Brown tosses out a pitch before a game in the early 1900s. He won 188 games in 10 seasons with the Cubs.

Pfiester was 20–8 and Ed Reulbach was 19–4. Frank Chance was the best all-around hitter at .319 with 103 runs scored. But for all their talent, the Cubs were upset by the Chicago White Sox in the 1906 World Series. The Cubs hit just .196 in the Series.

The Cubs came back and won 107 games in 1907. Then they beat the Detroit Tigers in the World Series. The Cubs won four games and tied one. The Cubs' pitchers only gave up six runs in the five-game Series.

Spalding

Original Cubs manager/pitcher Al Spalding became even better known for his sporting goods company and the baseballs that bore his name. While playing, he ran the A. G. Spalding & Bros. company. In 1876, Spalding began supplying the NL with the "official" baseball. The Spalding name is still very connected with baseball.

CALL HIM CAP

Adrian "Cap" Anson was a national hero whose name adorned many retail products. He was one of the first true stars of the Chicago Cubs. During his 22 seasons with the team, Anson collected 3,012 of his 3,435 career hits. He batted .331 and had 1,880 runs batted in while in Chicago. He was so skilled that he still batted .335 at age 43. He also managed the team for 19 seasons, from 1879 to 1897.

When he was fired as manager, Anson blamed his players: "The team with which I started out was certainly good enough to win the pennant, or finish in the first rank. That it failed to do so can only be explained by the underhanded work by some of the players looking toward my downfall."

But Anson was no saint himself. He actively worked to bar African Americans from playing in the NL.

In 1908, the Cubs were tied with the New York Giants at the end of the season. They played a tiebreaker game on October 8 at New York's Polo Grounds. Brown outdueled the great Christy Mathewson 4–2 in the game. At the World Series, the Cubs again beat the Tigers, four games to one.

The Cubs returned to the World Series again in 1910. But this time they lost to the Philadelphia Athletics. The Cubs were again runners-up in the 1918 World Series. After a season shortened by World War I, the Cubs lost to the Boston Red Sox in that World Series. Boston's ace pitcher that year was a man named Babe Ruth. He would go on to become one of baseball's all-time greatest hitters.

Many decades later, the Cubs would still be trying to add another World Series title.

Wrigley Field, shown in 1932, opened on the North Side of Chicago in 1914. The Cubs have been playing there since 1916.

But at the time, fans had other things to worry about. In 1916, the Cubs moved from West Side Grounds into two-year-old Weeghman Park. Chicago restaurant owner Charles Weeghman had built the ballpark at Clark and Addison streets for his Federal League Chicago Whales in 1914.

In 1916, however, he headed a group of investors that bought the Cubs for $500,000. Among the investors was chewing-gum manufacturer William Wrigley Jr., who put in $100,000. The Wrigley impact would affect the Cubs—good and bad—for decades to come.

CHAPTER 3

THE CUBS' GOLDEN ERA

William Wrigley Jr. became the Cubs' majority owner in 1919. Wrigley was the owner of the Wrigley Co., the world's largest gum manufacturer. He spared no expense on the Cubs and his North Side ballpark.

Perhaps the most lasting effect Wrigley had on the Cubs was through the team's home ballpark. Wrigley changed the name of the Cubs' home stadium from Cubs Park to Wrigley Field in 1916, before he became majority owner. He also added a second deck to the stadium in 1926, increasing the capacity from 20,000 to 38,396.

Wrigley expected the ballpark to be flawless and fan friendly. He would even wear white gloves and brush his hands on railings to ensure the park was clean. Behind the scenes, Wrigley worked with team president Bill Veeck Sr. to build a winning team.

Catcher Gabby Hartnett arrived in 1922. Then first

William Wrigley Jr., shown in 1929, became majority owner of the Cubs in 1919. The team remained in his family until 1981.

baseman Charlie Grimm joined the Cubs in 1925. Outfielders Riggs Stephenson and Hack Wilson became Cubs in 1926. A competitive pitching staff formed around starters Charlie Root and Guy Bush. The Cubs hired manager Joe McCarthy to run the club for the 1926 season.

All the additions paid off. The Cubs became a competitive team, just behind the powerful New York Giants. In the 1927 season, they were also the first team in the NL to draw more than 1 million fans. Several crowds at individual games passed the 45,000 mark.

To become the best, the Cubs went after the best hitter in the NL. On November 7, 1928, the Cubs traded five players and paid $200,000—a huge figure for the time—to the Boston Braves for Rogers Hornsby. At the time, he had a lifetime average of .361 with 2,476 hits, including 238 home runs. He instantly made the Cubs a top team in the NL.

Hornsby batted .380 with 39 homers in 1929. Meanwhile, Wilson hit 39 homers and 159 runs batted in (RBIs). The Cubs finished 98–54 and won their first pennant in 11 years by 10½ games. They were a success at the gate, too. The Cubs set a major league record when 1,485,166 fans attended games at Wrigley Field. That mark stood until 1946, when the New

Hack Wilson

Hack Wilson was called "the fireplug built like a man" for his 5-foot-6, 190-pound build. That body generated a lot of power. Wilson hit 177 homers in five seasons, from 1926 to 1930. However, the league made some changes to limit offense after an offensive surge in 1930. After that, Wilson declined to just 13 homers in 1931. He was later traded to the Brooklyn Dodgers.

Rogers Hornsby hits a single during a 1930 game. He won the NL Most Valuable Player Award in 1929.

York Yankees drew more than 2.2 million.

However, the Cubs met their match in the 1929 World Series. After losing the first two games to the Philadelphia Athletics, the Cubs came back to win Game 3 at Shibe Park in Philadelphia. Then disaster struck. The Cubs led 8–0 in the seventh inning of Game 4. But the A's tallied 10 runs in the bottom of the seventh. They were helped when Wilson lost two fly balls in the sun. The A's won the game and won the World Series two days later.

With their strong lineup intact, the Cubs were considered

A VETERAN CUB

Phil Cavarretta signed with the Cubs right out of high school in 1934. The first baseman/outfielder went on to have the longest career as a Cub after Adrian "Cap" Anson—parts of 20 seasons through 1953. He had 1,927 hits with a .292 average as a Cub. Although he was the NL's Most Valuable Player in 1945, his greatest moment took place on September 25, 1935. At Sportsman's Park in St. Louis, a 19-year-old Cavarretta slugged a homer that stood up as the only run in a 1–0 victory.

"The Good Lord must have been on my side," Cavarretta said. "I just wanted to get on base, and here I hit it out. I was on Cloud Nine going around the bases. It was the biggest hit I ever got."

The victory was crucial as the Cubs came from behind against the Cardinals. The Cubs were amid a 21-game winning streak to win the pennant.

favorites again in 1930. Wilson had one of the greatest seasons in history with 56 homers and 191 RBIs. His RBI total remains an MLB record. However, Hornsby was out for nearly four months due to injuries. Although the Cubs once had a 5½ game lead, they fell out of first place in September.

Hornsby replaced McCarthy as manager in 1930. But the move backfired. McCarthy became the Yankees' manager and led them to eight pennants in the 1930s and 1940s. Meanwhile, Hornsby proved to be a poor manager. He alienated his players with a nasty personality.

Hornsby was fired after Wrigley's death in 1932. Wrigley's son, Philip K. Wrigley, hired easygoing first baseman Grimm as a mid-season replacement. The Cubs went 37–18 under Grimm to win the

Hack Wilson, shown in 1930, led the NL in home runs during four of his first five seasons with the Cubs, beginning in 1926.

pennant again. That proved to be the end of the glory for 1932. The Yankees swept the Cubs in the World Series. Babe Ruth's famed "called-shot" home run in Game 3 at Wrigley Field turned into a sports legend. On the play, Ruth supposedly pointed toward center field before hitting a home run there.

The Cubs had established themselves as one of the top

The Called Shot

Almost every witness at Game 3 of the 1932 World Series, plus a home video, testified to Babe Ruth holding up two fingers, signaling "two strikes," to the Cubs dugout. However, popular lore says he pointed to the stands to call his homer. The Yankees won the game, 7–5.

teams in baseball. As such, they had many memorable seasons in the following years. In 1935, the Cubs won 21 straight games. That streak is second only to the Giants' 26-game winning streak in 1916. After being down 10½ games in July, the Cubs finished 100–54, four games ahead of the St. Louis Cardinals. However, they lost to the Tigers in six games in the World Series.

In 1938, the Cubs came from behind in the pennant race and tied the front-running Pittsburgh Pirates on September 28. Player/manager Gabby Hartnett came to bat with two outs and the score tied in the bottom of the ninth.

As darkness fell on Wrigley Field, the game would be called and would have to be replayed in its entirety if Hartnett did not do something. He did. Hartnett slugged a game-winning home run as the Cubs took over first place.

"I swung with everything I had, and then got that feeling when the blood rushes out of your head and you get dizzy," Hartnett said. "A lot of people told me they didn't know the ball was in the bleachers. I did. I knew it the minute I hit it."

Hartnett headed a victory parade in downtown Chicago a few days after the Cubs won their fourth pennant in ten years. But the same fate as before awaited them in the World Series. The Yankees swept them. The Cubs then declined over the next six years, fielding losing teams during World War II.

However, in 1945 the Cubs finished 98–56 and found themselves back in the World Series. But World Series disaster struck again. Cubs right-handed pitcher Claude

Cubs manager Gabby Hartnett looks on as his team plays the New York Yankees in the 1938 World Series.

Passeau threw a one-hitter against the Tigers in Game 3. The Series went to Game 7 at Wrigley Field. But Cubs pitcher Hank Borowy had been worn down by the time he took the mound in a 9–3 loss. After so much success, few would have thought that the Cubs would still, through 2013, be waiting for their next World Series appearance.

CHAPTER 4

THE SECOND WRIGLEY

The Cubs had been a team on the decline before the 1945 World Series. Philip K. Wrigley had taken over ownership of the team when his father died in 1932. William Wrigley Jr. had been more passionate about baseball than his son. But Philip promised his father that he would never sell the Cubs or Wrigley Field as long as he was financially able to maintain them.

The Cubs' problems began in 1933 when president William Veeck Sr. died. Veeck's replacements were not as successful. Before the 1945 pennant, the Cubs had five losing seasons. After the 1945 pennant, the Cubs had just one season above .500 through 1967.

The younger Wrigley often struggled with baseball and personnel decisions. He also had some innovative but misguided ideas. Wrigley, for example, did not believe the Cubs needed a farm system. A farm system is a group of minor league teams where players develop into

Cubs owner Philip K. Wrigley takes batting practice during spring training in the 1930s.

WHERE ARE THE LIGHTS?

Philip K. Wrigley had planned to install lights at Wrigley Field in 1942, but instead donated the steel for the light towers to the government after World War II. As the only team without lights, the Cubs had to play most of their games during the day. Some people believed that was partly to blame for the team's struggles.

Cubs trainer Gary Nicholson compiled an informal survey about how the all-day game schedule at Wrigley Field in the mid-1970s hurt the team's play. But Nicholson was told to keep his findings under wraps in order to protect Wrigley's order to not put in lights.

"Everybody sort of conceded it was correct, but nothing was ever going to happen, so nothing was to be gained by making a big deal about it," said then-Cubs media relations director Chuck Shriver. Wrigley Field finally got lights in 1988.

major leaguers. It was not until rivals like the St. Louis Cardinals and Brooklyn Dodgers had well-established farm systems that the Cubs finally created one in the 1940s. In 1948, the Cubs were the only team in the majors without lights on their stadium. That meant they had to play all of their home games during the hot summer days.

Then, in 1961, Wrigley instituted a "college of coaches" system. He wanted a group of coaches to rotate in and out of the manager job. They also worked in the minor leagues. He believed this would help unite the organization under one philosophy. But few around the league agreed with his plan. "If Mr. Wrigley wants to have eight coaches and no manager, that's strictly his business," said MLB Commissioner Ford Frick.

Ralph Kiner bats for the Cubs in 1953. He was a five-time All-Star with the Pittsburgh Pirates but could not help the Cubs become winners.

The Cubs' problems were obvious in the way young outfielder Lou Brock was managed. When he came up to the majors in 1961, one coach told him to drag bunt. Another suggested he swing for the fences. Without a true authority, Brock's development was slower than expected.

By 1964 he was finally beginning to look like a future star. Then the Cubs traded him to the Cardinals for pitcher Ernie Broglio. In St. Louis, Brock developed into the game's best base stealer, collected more than 3,000 hits, and was later elected into the Hall of Fame. Broglio had elbow surgery after the 1964 season and was released in 1966.

Through those dark seasons was one very bright spot. Shortstop Ernie Banks broke in with the Cubs in 1953. He was the team's first African-American player. He also turned out to be perhaps the Cubs' best player ever.

The skinny shortstop had quick wrists that generated surprising power. Banks had 41 or more home runs in five different seasons. He was named the NL's Most Valuable Player (MVP) in 1958 and 1959, even though the Cubs finished fifth during each season. Before retiring in 1971, Banks had hit 512 career home runs. He ended his career as one of the Cubs' most beloved players. The fans and media even began calling him "Mr. Cub."

Gene Baker

Although Ernie Banks is credited with being the first African American to play for the Cubs, his double-play partner Gene Baker nearly held that honor. Baker was a veteran shortstop in the Negro Leagues. He played four seasons with the Cubs' Triple-A team from 1950 to 1953. Many believed he was good enough to play in the majors during that time, but the Cubs controversially never brought him up. Finally, in 1953, the Cubs signed Banks and brought up Baker. Baker switched to second base upon Banks' arrival.

In the early 1960s, third baseman Ron Santo and outfielder Billy Williams joined Banks and the Cubs. The three players made for a powerful slugging trio. But they still could not turn the team into a winner. Finally, in 1965, Wrigley decided to make some drastic changes. In October, he gave up

Ernie Banks was twice the NL MVP during his 19 seasons in Chicago. He was enshrined in the Hall of Fame in 1977.

on the "college of coaches" and hired controversial manager Leo Durocher.

Durocher had won pennants with other teams. But he was also well known for often being mean and ornery. His most famous saying was, "Nice guys finish last." He even said he would trip his own grandmother to stop her from scoring a run.

The new manager vowed to make changes. But he first had to suffer through a 103-loss first season in 1966. The Cubs dramatically improved to 87–74 and third place in 1967. When they finished third again in 1968, many felt the Cubs were ready to make a pennant run.

The 1969 team jumped out to an early lead. The Cubs even had a 10-game lead over the New York Mets at one point in August. But then the lead slowly began melting away.

Durocher had an old-fashioned approach. He believed his starting lineup was his best way to win. So he played his regulars every day in the all-day game schedule. By early September the Cubs were wearing out just as the Mets were heating up. The Cubs won just eight of their final 26 games and finished second in the NL East.

The Cubs continued to contend for the next two seasons. But the players came into increasing conflict with Durocher. He struggled to understand the modern player. Durocher was fired midway through the 1972 season.

By the end of 1973, the Cubs' star players had aged. Some were traded away as the team sought to rebuild. There was little hope for the near future, either. The team's farm system continued to struggle in developing good, young players.

Bruce Sutter used his signature split-fingered fastball to become the first NL reliever to win the Cy Young Award in 1979.

In 1977, Philip K. Wrigley died at age 82. He passed the team on to his son, Bill Wrigley. The Cubs made an unexpected run at first place that year. They were 47–22 with an eight-game lead on June 29. But they again collapsed in the heat of the summer and finished 81–81.

As the league transitioned into an era of free agency, Bill Wrigley was unwilling to spend the money needed to lure star players to Chicago. With the Cubs sinking back into a losing atmosphere, the Wrigley era was coming to a close.

CHAPTER 5

COMING CLOSE, AGAIN

Soon after taking over the Cubs, Bill Wrigley found himself in financial trouble. Not wanting to risk selling his gum company, Wrigley quietly put the Cubs up for sale. But he wanted to avoid having people bid on the team. Instead, he offered it to his longtime broadcast partner, the Tribune Company.

The Tribune Company owned WGN-TV and WGN radio. WGN had broadcast Cubs games on TV since 1948 and on the radio since 1958. To keep those rights, Tribune bought the team in 1981. Changes began immediately. By the end of the 1981 season, the team had new management.

Daily Double

In 1984, Cubs leadoff hitter Bob Dernier and No. 2 hitter Ryne Sandberg were nicknamed the "Daily Double." Dernier had 45 stolen bases and Sandberg 32. They helped the Cubs score an NL-best 762 runs. Dernier never repeated his great season, but Sandberg only got better on his way to the Hall of Fame. He was inducted in 2005.

Cubs second baseman Ryne Sandberg, shown in 1994, was a 10-time All-Star and the 1984 NL MVP. He played 15 seasons with the Cubs.

The Cubs still struggled in 1982 and 1983. But they caught fire in 1984. The team added outfielders Gary Matthews and Bob Dernier, as well as pitchers Rick Sutcliffe and Dennis Eckersley in trades. Sutcliffe went 16–1 after joining the team midseason. Meanwhile, young second baseman Ryne Sandberg starred en route to winning the NL's MVP Award.

The Cubs won the NL East with 96 victories—the team's first championship of any kind since the 1945 NL pennant. They also drew 2 million fans for the first time.

The Cubs were favored over the San Diego Padres in the NLCS. After winning both games in Chicago, they needed just one win in San Diego to reach the World Series. But the Cubs were overconfident and lost the next three games. They even held a 3–0 lead going into the bottom of the sixth in Game 5 before falling short again.

The optimism entering the 1985 season faded when a 13-game losing streak in June and a series of injuries derailed the repeat effort. At one point in August, all five starting pitchers were on the disabled list. The Cubs did not recover in 1986. Free agent right fielder Andre Dawson won the MVP Award in 1987. He hit 49 home runs and had 137 RBIs. But the Cubs fell apart again.

By 1988, the Cubs' improved farm system began producing star players. Among them were pitcher Greg Maddux, first baseman Mark Grace, shortstop Shawon Dunston, catcher Joe Girardi, and outfielders Jerome Walton and Dwight Smith. Walton became the 1989 NL Rookie of the Year.

Boosted by veterans Dawson, Sandberg, and Sutcliffe,

Andre Dawson follows through on a two-run homer during a 1989 game against the Philadelphia Phillies.

the 1989 Cubs surprised by winning the NL East with 93 wins. However, that season came to another quick end when the Cubs lost to the San Francisco Giants in the NLCS. That 1989 season turned out to be the high point for that era of Cubs.

Maddux went 20–11 with a 2.18 ERA in 1992. He allowed just seven home runs in 268 innings. But the Cubs allowed him to leave as a free agent that off-season. Maddux became a staple of the Atlanta Braves' NL East dominance in the 1990s, while the Cubs pitching staff struggled.

In 1994, the Cubs hired Andy MacPhail as team president. He had been the Minnesota Twins' general manager when they won the 1987 and 1991 World Series titles. But the Cubs continued to struggle.

CHAPTER 6

STILL TRYING TO GET BACK

Although the Cubs struggled in the standings, the fans found reason to get excited. The Cubs had acquired outfielder Sammy Sosa in 1992. He had hit 33 home runs in his second season on the North Side. Then he belted 36 in 1995 and 40 in 1996. His production dramatically jumped in 1998.

Sosa gained national recognition when he hit 20 home runs in June. As the season continued, both Sosa and St. Louis Cardinals slugger Mark McGwire looked like they might break the single-season home-run record of 61. McGwire led the charge, but the duel caught the nation's attention.

"To me, I'm a winner already," Sosa said after he hit his 58th homer, still trailing McGwire. "I've gone so far this year and a lot more [home runs] are going to come. To me, just being behind Mark McGwire is being a winner."

McGwire finished with 70 home runs. But Sosa won the

Cubs slugger Sammy Sosa does his signature hop as he watches a home run sail away during the 1998 season.

NL MVP Award and finished with 66 home runs and 158 RBIs. The Cubs were also in the pennant race. They beat the Giants in a tie-breaking 163rd game to make the playoffs as the wild-card team.

Rookie pitcher Kerry Wood and his 99 miles-per-hour fastball played a huge role for the Cubs that season. On May 6, Wood made history by striking out his age. Wood, 20, tied the major league record with 20 strikeouts against the Houston Astros in a one-hit 2–0 victory. His breaking pitch was especially hard to make contact with on that rainy day in Chicago.

But Wood was injured during the final month of the season. He came back and started Game 3 of the NLDS against the Atlanta Braves. Still, the Braves swept the Cubs in three games. The Cubs struggled again in the next two

Slammin' Sammy

Sammy Sosa wasn't always a 60-home-run power hitter built like a linebacker. His nickname with the White Sox in the early 1990s was "The Panther" because of his sleek build. He wore gold chains early on as a Cub that showcased the numbers "30-30," signifying his goal of 30 homers and 30 stolen bases. Sosa achieved those numbers in 1993 with 33 homers and a career-high 36 steals. The only other time he got to that level was 1995, when he had 36 homers and 34 steals.

seasons. They made a first-place run into August of 2001 before having another poor season in 2002.

Sosa continued to put up giant power numbers. From 1999 to 2002, he hit 63, 50, 64, and 49 home runs. But soon his slugging feats came into question. Allegations of steroid use among players surfaced throughout MLB. Sosa stayed with the Cubs through their heartbreaking 2003 playoff

Pitcher Greg Maddux returned to the Cubs from 2004 to 2006 after spending 11 seasons with the Atlanta Braves.

run. But the Cubs traded him after the 2004 season.

The Cubs contended in 2004 but missed the playoffs. They struggled in 2005 and 2006 as top pitchers Wood and Mark Prior faced injuries. After the 2006 season, manager Dusty Baker was let go and president Andy MacPhail resigned.

New team president John McDonough oversaw the beginning of a new era on the North Side. He signed high-priced free agents like left fielder Alfonso Soriano and pitcher Ted Lilly. He also brought in respected—but fiery—manager Lou Piniella. McDonough was sick of the losing.

After a slow start in 2007, the Cubs won the NL Central Division with an 85–77 record. They were favored against the young Arizona Diamondbacks in the NLDS. But they lost in a three-game sweep.

Still, Piniella's first season was encouraging. The Cubs were favored to win the division again in 2008. They benefited early on from patience at the plate and great defense in right field from Kosuke Fukudome. Catcher and home run hitter Geovany Soto was headed for NL Rookie of the Year. With a 20–6 run to start August, the Cubs boosted their record to 85–50. No Cubs team had been that high above .500 since the 1945 pennant-winning team.

The Cubs finished 2008 with 97 wins—the most since 1945—and faced the Los Angeles Dodgers in the NLDS. But the Cubs lost two games at Wrigley Field. The Dodgers completed the sweep at home in Game 3. Once again, the Cubs came up empty in the postseason.

"I'm sure some guys were too amped up for their own good," said one longtime NL executive. "Some guys were not prepared mentally. You've got to treat it with some sense of urgency."

In October 2009, the Tribune Company sold the Cubs to the Ricketts family. The Ricketts were three brothers and a sister who sat for decades

Hot, Hot, Hot

Alfonso Soriano suffered a serious calf injury in early August 2007. But he came back just three weeks later to have his hottest month ever as a Cub. Soriano set a team record with 14 home runs in September, helping the team clinch the NL Central title. He beat Ernie Banks's record set in 1957.

Cubs outfielder Kosuke Fukudome waits for a pitch in a 2010 game against the Cincinnati Reds.

as loyal fans in the bleachers. Piniella retired in 2010. Numerous changes in the front office followed.

In 2011, Aramis Ramirez won a Silver Slugger Award. The next year, second baseman Darwin Barney won a Gold Glove.

Still, the team saw its fourth consecutive losing season in 2013. Yet as fans celebrated 100 years of Wrigley Field in 2014, they remained optimistic that the Cubs will one day break the curse and get back to the World Series.

TIMELINE

1876	The Cubs begin play as the Chicago White Stockings on April 25.
1879	Adrian "Cap" Anson becomes player-manager, and the most prominent team personality, through 1897.
1906	The Cubs win a major league record 116 games, but lose to the "Hitless Wonder" White Sox in the World Series on October 14.
1908	The Cubs capture their last World Series championship against the Detroit Tigers on October 14.
1914	Wrigley Field opens as Weeghman Park. The Cubs move in for the 1916 season, playing their first game on April 20.
1919	William Wrigley Jr. becomes majority Cubs owner. William Veeck Sr. serves as team president.
1929	The Cubs blow an 8–0 lead and give up 10 runs in Game 4 of the World Series to the Philadelphia Athletics on October 12, eventually losing in five games.
1932	William Wrigley Jr. dies at 70 on January 26, and is succeeded by son Philip K. Wrigley as owner.
1932	The Cubs are swept four in a row by the New York Yankees in the World Series, which includes Babe Ruth's "called-shot" home run on October 1.
1935	The Cubs win 21 in a row in September to overtake the St. Louis Cardinals and win the pennant, but lose the World Series to the Detroit Tigers in six games.

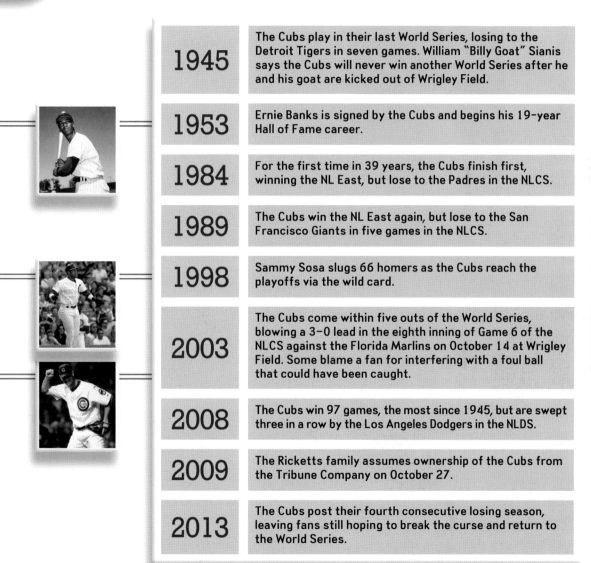

1945 — The Cubs play in their last World Series, losing to the Detroit Tigers in seven games. William "Billy Goat" Sianis says the Cubs will never win another World Series after he and his goat are kicked out of Wrigley Field.

1953 — Ernie Banks is signed by the Cubs and begins his 19-year Hall of Fame career.

1984 — For the first time in 39 years, the Cubs finish first, winning the NL East, but lose to the Padres in the NLCS.

1989 — The Cubs win the NL East again, but lose to the San Francisco Giants in five games in the NLCS.

1998 — Sammy Sosa slugs 66 homers as the Cubs reach the playoffs via the wild card.

2003 — The Cubs come within five outs of the World Series, blowing a 3–0 lead in the eighth inning of Game 6 of the NLCS against the Florida Marlins on October 14 at Wrigley Field. Some blame a fan for interfering with a foul ball that could have been caught.

2008 — The Cubs win 97 games, the most since 1945, but are swept three in a row by the Los Angeles Dodgers in the NLDS.

2009 — The Ricketts family assumes ownership of the Cubs from the Tribune Company on October 27.

2013 — The Cubs post their fourth consecutive losing season, leaving fans still hoping to break the curse and return to the World Series.

QUICK STATS

FRANCHISE HISTORY

Chicago White Stockings (1876–89)
Chicago Colts (1890–97)
Chicago Orphans (1898–1902)
Chicago Cubs (1903–)

WORLD SERIES
(wins in bold)

1906, **1907**, **1908**, 1910, 1918, 1929,
1932, 1935, 1938, 1945

NL CHAMPIONSHIP SERIES
(1969–)

1984, 1989, 2003

DIVISION CHAMPIONSHIPS
(1969–)

1984, 1989, 2003, 2007, 2008

KEY PLAYERS
(position[s]; seasons with team)

Ernie Banks (SS/1B; 1953–71)
Phil Cavarretta (1B/OF; 1934–53)
Andre Dawson (OF; 1987–92)
Gabby Hartnett (C; 1922–41)
Fergie Jenkins (SP; 1966–73; 1982–83)
Ryne Sandberg (2B; 1982–94;
   1996–97)
Ron Santo (3B; 1960–73)
Lee Smith (RP; 1980–87)
Sammy Sosa (OF; 1992–2004)
Rick Sutcliffe (SP; 1984–91)
Billy Williams (OF/1B; 1959–74)
Hack Wilson (OF; 1926–31)

KEY MANAGERS

Cap Anson (1879–97):
   1,283–932
Charlie Grimm (1932–38; 1944–49,
   1960): 946–782; 5–12 (postseason)

HOME PARKS

23rd Street Grounds (1876–77)
Lakefront Park (1878–84)
West Side Park (1885–91)
South Side Park (1891–93)
West Side Grounds (1893–1915)
Wrigley Field (1916–)

* All statistics through 2013 season

QUOTES AND ANECDOTES

The Cubs have not been no-hit since Sandy Koufax threw a perfect game against them in Dodger Stadium on September 9, 1965. But that game was historic for more than just that fact. The fewest number of hits ever in a game—one—was recorded. Cubs pitcher Bob Hendley allowed that one hit—a bloop double by Lou Johnson in the seventh—that had nothing to do with the run. Both pitchers had no-hitters going into the seventh, but the Dodgers scored an unearned run in the fifth on a throwing error by catcher Chris Krug. "Although it hurts to know you lost, I still had a good feeling about it," Hendley said. "You knew you were part of something special. The hurt was probably a little lessened."

Cubs catcher Chris Krug went on to become a builder of baseball fields. He constructed perhaps the most famous field ever in movies. He carved the diamond out of a Dyersville, Iowa, cornfield for the 1989 movie *Field of Dreams*.

On June 30, 1959, two baseballs were accidentally put into play at the same time in a game between the Cubs and Cardinals at Wrigley Field. A ball four to Cardinals batter Stan Musial in the fourth inning got away from catcher Sammy Taylor and rolled back near the screen. Time was not called by plate ump Vic Delmore. Musial ran to first, then continued to second because time was not called. Delmore pulled another ball from his pocket and gave it to Taylor. He noticed Musial running to second and overthrew second in an attempt to nab him. Meanwhile, Cubs third baseman Alvin Dark retrieved the original ball behind the plate, saw Musial and threw that ball toward shortstop Ernie Banks, who tagged out Musial. The Cardinals protested the confusing play, but it wasn't needed as they won 4–1. "A comedy of errors," said Anderson. "Only with the Cubs at that time could something like that happen."

GLOSSARY

bleachers

Uncovered seats in a ballpark's outfield, often without backs or arm rests.

box seats

The most expensive seats in a ballpark, closest to the infield.

doubleheader

Two games played in the same ballpark on the same day.

farm system

A big-league club's teams in the minor leagues, where players are developed for the majors.

free agent

A player whose contract has expired and who is able to sign with a team of his choice.

general manager

The executive who is in charge of the team's overall operation. He or she hires and fires managers and coaches, drafts players, and signs free agents.

pennant

A flag. In baseball, it symbolizes that a team has won its league championship.

postseason

The games in which the best teams play after the regular-season schedule has been completed.

retire

To officially end one's career.

rookie

A first-year player in the major leagues.

wild card

Playoff berths given to the best remaining teams that did not win their respective divisions.

FOR MORE INFORMATION

Further Reading

Holtzman, Jerome, and George Vass. *The Cubs Encyclopedia*. Philadelphia, PA: Temple University Press, 1997.

Vorwald, Bob. *Cubs Forever: Memories from the Men Who Lived Them*. Chicago: Triumph Books, 2008.

Wisnia, Saul. *Chicago Cubs Yesterday & Today*. Lincolnwood, IL: West Side Pub., 2008.

Websites

To learn more about Inside MLB, visit **booklinks.abdopublishing.com**. These links are routinely monitored and updated to provide the most current information available.

Places to Visit

Cubs Park

2330 W. Rio Salado Parkway
Mesa, AZ 85201
480-668-0500
chicago.cubs.mlb.com/chc/mesa/
Cubs Park became the Cubs' spring-training ballpark in 2014.

National Baseball Hall of Fame and Museum

25 Main Street
Cooperstown, NY 13326
1-888-HALL-OF-FAME
www.baseballhall.org
This hall of fame and museum highlights the greatest players and moments in the history of baseball. Ernie Banks, Ryne Sandberg, and Hack Wilson are among the former Cubs enshrined there.

Wrigley Field

1060 W. Addison St.
Chicago, IL 60613
773-404-CUBS
mlb.mlb.com/chc/ballpark/index.jsp
This has been the Cubs' home field since 1916. The team plays 81 regular-season games here each year. Tours are available.

INDEX

About the Author

George Castle grew up on Chicago's North Side, five miles northwest of Wrigley Field. He used to pay $1 to attend games in the right-field bleachers and $1.75 in the grandstands. He has covered the Cubs for media outlets since 1980. Castle has authored 11 baseball books since 1998, hosts the syndicated weekly "Diamond Gems" radio show, and writes for a variety of print and online outlets.